Destiny

ALSO BY NGOZI OLIVIA OSUOHA

The Transformation Train
Letter to My Unborn
Sensation
Tropical Escape (with Amos O. Ojwang')
Fruits from the Poetry Planet
Poetic Grenade
Whispers of the Biafran Skeleton
Chains
Raindrops
Freeborn
Eclipse of Tides
The Subterfuge
Green Snake on a Green Grass
Chariots of Archangels
Wonderment
Interwoven
xenophobicracy
The Phenomenal Human

Destiny

poems by
Ngozi Olivia Osuoha

Poetic Justice Books
Port St. Lucie, Florida

©2020 Ngozi Olivia Osuoha

book design and layout: SpiNDec, Port Saint Lucie, FL
cover image: *Looking Away*, ©2017 Kris Haggblom

All rights reserved.

No part of this book may be used or reproduced in any manner whatsoever without written permission except in the case of brief quotations embodied in critical articles and reviews. Members of educational institutions and organizations wishing to photocopy any of the work for classroom use, or authors, artists and publishers who would like to obtain permission for any material in the work, should contact the publisher.

Printed in the United States of America.
Published by Poetic Justice Books
Port Saint Lucie, Florida
www.poeticjusticebooks.com

ISBN: 978-1-950433-41-4

FIRST EDITION
10 9 8 7 6 5 4 3 2 1

*This poetry book is dedicated to
God, the destiny moulder.*

contents

DESTINY	3
DREAM	4
VISION	5
FRIENDSHIP	6
DESTINED	7
DESTINY'S CHILD	8
COMPANION	9
SPOUSE	10
ROLE MODEL	11
GOD	12
BELIEF	13
DELAY	14
SCHOOL	15
EDUCATION	16
NATIVITY	17
CULTURE	18
FAMILY	19
CHARACTER	20
DISTANCE	21
FATE	22
COINCIDENCE	23
TIME	24
CALLING	25
PASSION	26
CRAFT	27
LOYALTY	28
OBEDIENCE	29
HUMILITY	30
RESPECT	31
DILIGENCE	32

ACCOUNTABILITY	33
HONESTY	34
TRANSPARENCY	35
DEDICATION	36
COMMITMENT	37
CAREFULNESS	38
TRUTHFULNESS	39
TRUSTWORTHINESS	40
FORCES	41
TEMPTATION	42
TRIALS	43
DISTRACTION	44
HARDSHIP	45
STUMBLING BLOCK	46
HINDRANCE	47
DECEIT	48
FOCUS	49
WAYWARDNESS	50
UPS AND DOWNS	51
DIVINITY	52
ORDERLINESS	53
HAND OF GOD	54
DIRECTION	55
ENEMIES	56
FAKE FRIENDS	57
BETRAYERS	58
BAD RELATIVES	59
WRONG COMPANY	60
FAMILY OUTRAGE	61

MADNESS	62
RESTLESSNESS	63
INTEREST	64
LOVE	65
WANTS AND NEEDS	66
STRUGGLE	67
SERIOUSNESS	68
DETERMINATION	69
WATERING	70
LEARNING	71
GROWING	72
DISCOVERY	73
FORWARD MOVEMENT	74
RAPE	75
ACCIDENT	76
WITCHCRAFT AND WIZARDRY	77
HATE	78
WICKEDNESS	79
GOSSIP	80
SCANDAL	81
RUMOUR	82
BLACKMAIL	83
ILLITERACY	84
POVERTY	85
ROADBLOCKS	86
FRUSTRATIONS	87
ABANDONMENT	88
DISOWN	89
LONELINESS	90

DEPRESSION	91
ABUSE	92
FOOL	94
DOUBTS AND SELF DOUBTS	95
UNWANTED	96
HELPLESS	97
CONFUSION	98
BANDWAGON	99
PEER PRESSURE	100
DOGMAS	101
MENTALITY	102
TABOO	103
BROKE	104
CONNECTIONS AND GODFATHERS	105
FAVOUR AND FAME	106
DECISION	107
SCALE OF PREFERENCE	108
PRIORITY	109
ODDS AND PURPOSE	110
BREAKTHROUGH	111
VOICE	112
FORGONE ALTERNATIVE	113

Destiny

DESTINY

Destiny is divine
We come with it,
On our palms, inscribed
On our foreheads, marked
No matter what
However, wherever, whatever
Whatever happens
Wherever we go
Destiny finds us.

It holds on, it fights on
Destiny cheers up
It never succumbs,
Destiny is patient
It can ensure anything
Destiny accepts longsuffering
It never runs away
Destiny waits, it prays
It pleads and beckons
Destiny is a force, celestial.

Destiny can be delayed
It can be frustrated
Yet, whatever happens to destiny
Destiny just comes through.

Ngozi Olivia Osuoha

DREAM

There is a dream
That gives you peace
And keeps you restless too.

There is a dream
That makes you crazy
And joyful as well.

There is a dream
That fears you
But calms you down too.

There is a dream
That fills you with doubts
Yet, grants you freedom.

There is a dream
That creates ripples,
Yet, holds you hostage.

There is a dream
That breaks your limits
Yet, tears you apart.

Hold on to that dream
That is destiny
It troubles, it saves
It builds, it haunts
Until you face it,
Yet, it will not be that easy.

VISION

You see it clear
You long for it
You wish to have it
And you go for it,
You declare it
You talk about it
You tell of it
You are so sure
Though others may not.

A clear vision
Crystal like star
It brings lucidity
And vividly leads
It establishes facts
And prunes noises
It wards off nuisances
And ascertains the way
Yet, they may not believe it.

Vivid vision, rigorous
Vigorous, vital and vast
That is it, run it.

FRIENDSHIP

Friendship is natural
It is even in animals
Friendship helps a lot.

Friendship also guides destiny
Good friendship uplifts it
Bad friendship deters it.

Beware of friends, then
Tend to friendship
Bear the light
And seek the track.

Lift friends, mend their hearts
Remember, nobody is perfect
Two heads are better than one.

A great friend heals
A crooked friend, harms
Look out, watch out
Friendship is a path to destiny
Be friends with your destiny
So your destiny will shine forth.

DESTINED

People are born different
They bear marks, many
They take lanes, numerous
They fulfill missions, diverse
They are destined.

People are predestined
They come here for work
A specific job they do
Some find out
Some discover
Some actualize
Some rigmarole
Some while away time
And some never realize.

Destiny is sacred
It is ordained and consecrated
Discovered; fulfilled
Undiscovered; perambulating.

Look deep, wonder yonder
Search further, go farther
Your destiny will lead the world.

DESTINY'S CHILD

Listen, destiny's child
You are born to shine
Shine beyond stars,
So shine and keep shining.

Listen, destiny's child
You are born to rule
Rule beyond rulers,
So rule and keep ruling.

Hello, destiny's child
Look beyond worries
Forget your sorrows
These troubles will not last,
But you will do.

Hello, destiny's child
March on, move on, hold on
Destiny is looking for you
Routing, searching, advancing speedily,
Stay on your lane, focus.

Destiny prays for you
Destiny supports you
Be strong, hang in, there
Destiny's child, dig it up
You are more than a miner
You are gold, raw gold.

COMPANION

Destiny needs companionship
So beware of your company,
Destiny is a companion
Keep him company.

Companions vary, they are plenty
Good, bad, right, wrong
Be mindful of your destiny
Because it does not frolic with all.

Destiny overwhelms, overcomes
Be ready for turbulence
Whether on sea, land or air.

Destiny fights, destiny battles
Destiny baffles, destiny marvels
Be prepared for wonders.

Your destiny is green
Let it never lie fallow
Cultivate even the furrow
Fertilize the marrow
Even in the hollow of peace.

Ngozi Olivia Osuoha

SPOUSE

Spouse is necessary
It helps in life
But care must be taken
In choosing one.

Spouse helps, uplifts
Spouse makes a way
Forward, backward
Left, right, roundabout.

Spouse bears luck
Spouse carries grace
Spouse gives headway
Spouse brings peace
It depends on who,
And choice.

Spouse can drain
Spouse can pull you down
Spouse can make you crazy.

Destiny too, can be tied to spouse
Clear your eyes, see well
Look beyond cosmetics and makeups
Destiny is linked to a link
Spouse is a huge part too.

ROLE MODEL

Role models are many
They model whatever
To whoever,
And people follow them on.

Destiny needs a role model
The one to model you
To fine-tune and prune you
A focus, target, map.

Without them, destiny can live
Without them, destiny can survive
But they are a compass
A roadmap, and forest guide.

So be careful who models you
And who you model for,
One you follow or look up to
Wolves in sheep's clothing
Shepherds destroying flocks
Be careful, be watchful.

Role models do harm too
They are imperfect as well
Just like you, they fail and fall
Fish out divine ones for you
Let them strengthen your journey.

GOD

There is a Creator
Who created heaven and earth
He made man too
In His image and likeness.

He breathed into man
And gave him life
He inscribed his journey
And planted his mission
He put into him, vision
And called it destiny.

Destined, predestined, ordained
Fate, divine, divinity
It must happen.

Find this Creator
Run to Him
Lean on God
You will discover your purpose.

Live your purpose, destiny
Lead your destiny, purpose
Let the world witness it
Then your maker will be happy with you.

BELIEF

Belief is a force
It propels the living
And drives living too.

Belief is an arrow
It is packed in the quiver
It helps to hit a target
When rightly shot.

Belief is a light
A guiding light, shining
It disperses darkness.

Belief is a future
It brightens or darkens
Belief is a window or door
It allows entrance or exit.

Know what to believe
Know how to follow your belief,
Belief is tied to destiny
As destiny is tied to belief,
Both save or kill.

DELAY

Delay is the hand of time
It either stands still
Or moves backward
It can go anticlockwise, too.

Delay is always around
From whichever quarters
Either for us or against us.

But then, delay is temporary
It is not denial
Destiny can only be delayed.

Fear not the delays
Be not dismayed
Relent not, nor despair
For it is only but awhile.

Delay can be very discouraging
It can be painful
Very hurtful and deadly
But just hold on to your duty post
Destiny crushes delay.

SCHOOL

School is important
Where we get education
Different types, levels and grades.

We meet people there
Depending on our route
They come in many shades
Depending on their roles.

School, rich school
School, poor school
We learn, less or more.
Teachers, qualified and sound
Syllabus, rich and enough
Curriculum, great and small
We pass through them.

Yes, schools help destiny
Locations, specialities, time
All brush destinies.

Look well, choose well
Especially according to your means,
School and schooling refine us
They decide a part of our life too.

EDUCATION

Education is key
The key to many things
Education opens ways,
Ways and great doors
Doors locked by ignorance and illiteracy.

Education breaks chains
Yes, chains against destiny
It cuddles and couples destiny.

Education kisses civilization
It loves modernization
And embraces freedoms.

Education marries destiny
It weds missions and visions
Get education, be liberated.

Education is an Eye-opener
It gives sight to the blind
It motivates destiny
And inspires predestination,
Education helps the ordained.

NATIVITY

Nativity is natural
No one chooses his
The nativity of a man
Tells much of him.

It touches his destiny
It wraps it up
It may boost it
Or otherwise.

Destiny is nativity
It comes from birth
It does not need consent
It just comes.

We unfold it, or kill it
We discover it or bury it
We neither sell nor buy it
Destiny locates us at will.

Your native destiny
And the nativity of your destiny
All define and describe you.

CULTURE

Culture is our way of life
The way we do everything
People by people, time by time.

Culture is with destiny
They are intertwined
Interwoven, fresh or flesh
Sinking or floating
Culture loves destiny.

Destiny may be bright
Culture may be dark
Destiny may be dark
To do whatever mysterious,
And then culture will be bright
But these two are one.

Bright destiny brightens culture
Dark destiny darkens culture
Dark culture cannot brighten destiny
And dark destiny cannot brighten culture,
Rule your destiny
And brighten the world.

FAMILY

Family is destiny
Destiny is family
They are a couple
And they have couple effect.

Family affects destiny largely
Destiny influences family well
Hand in hand, together as one
They work wonders.

Great family supports destiny
Great people admire destinies
Real families propagate destiny
They unite, they fight, they lead.

Family is everything
Everything is family
Good or bad, better or worse
Family counts, family still counts
Family is all.

Support your family, in and out
Let your destiny germinate
Water your family all round
For there, is your divine settlement.

Ngozi Olivia Osuoha

CHARACTER

Character speaks volume
It tells who we are
It is not about cosmetics
Manmade and artificialities,
Character defines us.

Destiny is tied to character
We need soundness to be there
Destiny requires purity
It needs sanity
Bad character tangles destiny.

Character is all, everything
Good character paves way
As bad one hinders.

Destiny is character
Character is destiny,
Pure or impure
Rude or smart
Destiny requires gentility
Humility supports destiny
Live it, destiny is character.

DISTANCE

Distance is real
It can be short or long
But it obeys destiny.

Distance hearkens, listens
Tides of destiny shun distance
Because distance is not a barrier.

Destiny knows distance
Distance believes destiny
They both work together
They yield, they give in
Each of them understands.

Distance is productive
Destiny is positive,
Activity happens to them.

No matter the distance
Despite the destiny
When they are meant to be
They find each other,
They make way and time
They meet date and fate.

Ngozi Olivia Osuoha

FATE

Fate is a mystery
No one truly understands
It can be anyhow
It can flow any way
Fate is a wonder.

It is destiny too
But bewilders, beclouds
Fate is a puzzle
It is full of amazement.

Destiny is a fate
Fate is a destiny
We pray it be good
Not evil, not ill, not horror.

Fate steps in and out
It goes back and forth
None really comprehends.

But destiny is there
Willing, agitating, pleading
Supplicating, supplying, saturating
Destiny is awesome,
From an awesome abode.

COINCIDENCE

Coincidences are wonders
They tell of a higher force
Their realm is unique.

Coincidences are puzzles
They make one lost,
Lost in amazement.

Destiny can be coincidental
Yet divinely arranged,
Programmed and fashioned
Beyond chances and times.

Coincidences are mysteries
Sometimes, they look suspicious
They tell fairy tales
They tell holy stories
Fancies, fantasies, fallacies
All and many more;
Perplexing, confusing.

Destiny is great and real
It goes far from coincidence,
Yet comes close to it.

TIME

Time is a phenomenon
It is slippery yet steady
Time is a river
It flows, yet never dries.

Time is destiny
It is ordained
It is timed
Tick, tock, tock, tick
It keeps ticking
It must come to pass.

Time is a guage
It measures destiny
Destiny is a metre
It rules time.

Destiny is time
Time is destiny
Rule, measure, check
Abide, obey, fit in
Let none slip away.

CALLING

We are called
We are chosen
Many are called
But few are chosen.

Called? answer
Chosen? work
Answer and work
For time passes away.

Callings are vast
Each man to his ability
Callings are great
Each one to his gift
To work for the caller
To serve the giver
To bless the gifted.

Answer your call
Know you call
For there, is your destiny
Choose wisely, obey
For obedience is better than sacrifice.

Know your caller
Be with Him,
Answer, and be blessed.

PASSION

Passion is a force
It is a propeller
A great locomotive
A big turbine
Driving the engine of our life.

Passion is a clothing
It clothes our nakedness
Passion is a shelter
It is the roof over our head
Passion is food
It satisfies our hunger
Passion quenches our thirst.

Destiny is passion
Passion is destiny
A passionate destiny saves
A destined passion serves.

Serve, save, work, bless
Your destiny is ordained
Keep it sacred and holy
Let the oil of consecration overrule.

CRAFT

Craft is there for man
It helps man fit in, too
Craft is of the hand
That which the hand, finds.

Diligence suffers, yes
But the most blessed
Faithfulness pays
Trust, sincerity, honesty
All, help craft.

Craft is a great gift
If you have it, treasure it
Craft is also destiny.

Destiny is a holy craft
Crafted to ward off evil,
Witchcraft can fight it
But craftsmen never relent.

Destiny is huge and large
Nothing threatens it more than self,
Be ready, be prepared
Be consistent, it will happen.

LOYALTY

Loyalty is a feather
It sits on destiny's cap
Standing tall, elegant
Like an eagle, proud.

Loyalty respects destiny
As destiny appreciates it too.

Destiny is loyal to loyalty
Destiny advances, metamorphosing
With an empirical formula
Moving in honour for honour.

Loyalty is destiny
For only destiny can be loyal
North, south, east, west
Home is destiny, destiny is home.

Loyalty appreciates, values
Destiny grows, multiplies
Both elevate one another
With a green compliment
Reaching home to the Creator.

OBEDIENCE

Obedience is a virtue
Not everyone obeys.

Obedience is a character
Not all know it.

Obedience is an honour
It lifts, it belittles.

Obedience paves way
Even in the desert.

Obedience speaks to destiny
Even in the wilderness.

Obedience obeys destiny
Destiny hears obedience
Both understand each other.

Destiny prunes obedience
Obedience levels destiny,
They augment, compliment
Because the diviner made it so.

HUMILITY

Humility stands the test of time
It exaults destiny,
And uplifts the predestined.

Humility compensates
And advocates
Humility is destiny
And destiny is humble.

The humbleness of destiny
And the humility of destiny
Both cook pride
The pride for next generation.

Destiny is a humble ground
It grows diverse seeds
Its fertility is beyond measure.

Humility loves its destiny
Riches cannot buy it
Humility entices destiny,
Pomposity dares not
Be humble, for destiny is poor
And humble, no matter what.

RESPECT

Respect is reciprocal
Everyone loves to be respected
Even when they do not deserve it.

Respect is universal
Old and young, men and women
Children and youth,
Everyone clamours for it.

Destiny deserves much respect
Because it is foundational
Misinterpreted, we are lost
Misunderstood, we are gone
Mistreated, we are finished
Mistrusted, we regret it
Destiny must be respected.

Respect is the final point
It is a cooking pot
It serves the rich and the poor
But some destroy the pot.

Table, respect destiny
For destiny is the table of life
Sit there then, and be fed.

DILIGENCE

Diligence is the bedrock of work
Without it, one is lost
No matter the fast lane
And the trickish lifestyle.

Pranks and tricks quench
They slow down and die
They fade suddenly or gradually
But diligence never does.

Tie your destiny to diligence
Because the two are one.

Diligence always comes back
Searching for the faithful servant
Even when he is long gone
His generations partake in it.

Destiny is diligent
It delights too,
It works timely, gradually
Faithfully, honestly, loyally
Fearfully, trustworthily, forever
Even when all things are parallel.

ACCOUNTABILITY

Accountability is self probe
It watches self for others.

Accountability is transparency
It mirrors self and others.

Destiny is accountability
Without it, it is lost
Without it, it is extravagant
Without it, it achieves nothing.

Destiny is accountable to nature
Destiny is accountable to his creator
Time, date, season, within, without
Destiny accounts for everything.

Accountability sustains destiny
Without which imprudence leads
Destiny is attached to it
For self denial, self discipline
Self respect, self esteem and freedom.

Define yourself, define your destiny
Let accountability never miss,
Lest you miss all.

Ngozi Olivia Osuoha

HONESTY

Honesty is a watchword
It is a motto
And a slogan
Honesty is a virtue
Anyone who posses it, is rich
No matter what comes.

Honesty twinkles destiny
It showcases it well
It brings it to limelight
And sustains it there.

Honesty is a lamp
It shines brighter
Darkness fears it
Gloominess respects it,
Honesty is a crown
It enthrones real people.

Destiny is honest
It does not lie nor deceive
Truth is destiny
Destiny is truth
 Honesty, truth and truthfulness
Those boost destiny,
Stay glued to them.

TRANSPARENCY

Transparency is a foundation
Building on it, is firm
Strong foundations last
Weak ones crash.

Transparency helps destiny
It stretches it so long
To get to utmost worlds.

Transparency is a coin
It guards the loin
And buys the lion.

Destiny is transparent
Nothing is hidden in it,
Especially when discovered.

Transparency is destiny
Destiny transpires
And transmits,
From walls to walls
From worlds to worlds
From walks to walks
From works to works
Destiny is clear.

DEDICATION

Be dedicated to destiny
Commit unto it
It will commit unto you.

Destiny requires dedication
It breaks bounds and bonds
It breaks limits and boundaries.

Barriers succumb and tumble
Dedication exhumes destiny
It escalates it
And treasures it forever.

Dedication is pure, it is golden
Selflessness and preparedness
Time, strength, energy, courage, bravery
Destiny works well with them all.

Dedication is to destiny
What air is to human
Breathe it, and live
Without it, it is death
Feed your destiny
Let it live beyond the earth.

COMMITMENT

Destiny is your family
Be committed to it.

Provide for it, cloth it, shelter it
Feed and water it,
Grow it with all your might
Let the bell of commitment ring
Blow the trumpet of work
Let the alarm keep you awake
So that you shall not slumber.

Commitment is a ladder
It helps destiny climb
It towers to the heavens
And showers like rain
Blessing the earth
And flourishing the flowers.

Commitment romances, dances
Destiny caresses commitment
Commit, commit, work and labour
Love and cherish, grow and tend
For only minders capture the world.

CAREFULNESS

Care is a great tool
It saves the world
Carelessness is a trap
It catches even the great.

Carefulness is a plus
It yields to movements,
And increases volumes.

Carefulness preserves destiny
And covers power
It enhances might
And upgrades strength.

Carefulness oils destiny
And lures growth
Carefulness is a builder
It raises up buildings
Buildings of hope and faith.

See that destiny survives
So that it never slip away
Guard and guide it
Let carefulness protect you, too.

TRUTHFULNESS

Destiny is fine and pure
It does not lie
It neither deceives nor cheats
Destiny is truthful.

Destiny works with truth
Truthfulness caps it
Destiny lurks for virtues
Truthfulness is one.

Being true, staying true
Living true, going true
All, improve destiny.

Destiny is destined truly
It does not abhor truthfulness
Destiny cherishes truth
They glue together.

Your destiny is true and truthful
But you may have to adjust
Yes, adjust and readjust
Adopt, adapt, reconsider.

TRUSTWORTHINESS

Trust is destiny
Because destiny is trustworthy
Tested and trusted
Trusted before birth.

Destiny creates trust
It closes doubts
Because it is real
Straight and straightforward.

Destiny builds trust
And dismantles distrust
Destiny urges frankness
And fans pureness.

Trust is a lamp
A headlamp and searchlight,
The hunter's headlamp
The miner's searchlight,
Destiny is them all.

FORCES

Destiny is a force
It pulls forces along,
And battles against forces also.

Destiny is a force
It opposes forces
And fights frictions.

Destiny is a force
It scores goals
And touches mountains.

Destiny rises up and down
Destiny falls deep and deep
Yet, it survives wars
And wins in the end.

Destiny is a force
A great bullet
It pulls triggers
And kills enemies.

Destiny is a force
It aligns us almost all the time,
We must learn to submit.

Ngozi Olivia Osuoha

TEMPTATION

Temptations abound
They come from anywhere
They come in many forms,
Fighting destiny to win.

Temptations want to crush
Yes, they come against destiny
They want it crushed
But destiny is stronger than pain.

Destiny suffering, choking
Temptations tempting
Struggling, strangling
Bewitching, setting up
But destiny is always prevailing.

Temptations of great forces
Pulling down giants
Crippling the mighty
Paralyzing the great.

Destiny is strong
Stronger than pain,
As strong as the Creator
The one who made it,
It wins, it wins, it does
Because the Creator is behind it.

TRIALS

Trials will come
Many clash with destiny
They fight to subdue it
But destiny is strong.

Trials, seen and unseen
Known and unknown
Light and heavy
Fair and unfair
Great and small
From any corner
Fighting, trying to suffocate destiny.

Trials sometimes help
 They wake some up
They strengthen some
They intimidate some, however.

Trials are like rope
They drag destiny
Towing it to wherever
But strong people cut it off
And pull themselves higher.

Focus on destiny
Not on trials,
Keep your head up
The God of destiny will win.

DISTRACTION

Distraction everywhere
Here and there, upside down
Physically, mentally, morally
Academically, socially, generally.

Distraction in various forms
Just to take destiny away
To cripple gifts and calls
To quench fires
Fires of passion and zeal.

Sidetrack them, sideline them
Distractions are forces
Forces of rare strength and intent
They pounce on destiny.

Sex, lust, drugs, waywardness
Indiscipline, selfishness, alcoholism,
More, moving in diverse methods
With designs and patterns
Some appearing like angels
Some in form of the best
But with the intent of crashing destiny.

Beware, be careful
Focus, be guided
Victory is achievable.

HARDSHIP

Yes, hardship is a tool
A tool that fights destiny.

Great destinies meet with hardship
They break and quench
Make and break, sideways
They tussle, hustle, and puzzle
And their muscles tire and wear out.

Hardship can be in any thing
Learning, living, growing
Feeding, expanding, working.

Hardship is a stumbling block
It blocks progress
It disrupts greatness
And hinders connections.

Hardship tries destiny
It tests its durability and ability
But determination pulls it down.

Destiny can be hardened too
Harden up, hammer it down
Success will splash everywhere.

STUMBLING BLOCK

Stumbling block
Stumbling blocks
They are many
In different sizes, shapes and shades.

Stumbling block
They are real
Home and abroad.

Stumbling block
They abound,
In job, job place
In love, love place
In work, work place
Everywhere, in and out.

Be careful
Find them,
Look out for them
Avoid them.

Stumbling block
A big threat to destiny
But destiny is a bigger threat
In fact, destiny threatens everything
So be strong, threaten back
Stay put, stay victorious.

HINDRANCE

Hindrance, hindrances
Hindrances, waging war
War against future
War against destiny.

Hindrances, forces large, small
Enemies of progress
Forces and counter forces.

Hindrances, thick and thin
Lean and fat
Weak and strong,
Pushing down strongholds
Strongholds of destiny.
Fear them not
Be bold, be courageous
Your destiny rocks and rolls
Row it beyond the waters.

Win the storm.
Silence the wave
Kill the tempest
You are mighty
Win all, win all destiny calls.

DECEIT

Deceit can kill
Yes, it can, it does.

Deceit from anywhere
Can hurt, can harm
Yes it can, it does.

Be wise, be smart
Be articulated, be alert
Deceivers abound
Even in holy robes.

Deceit deceives destiny
It kills the destined
It makes fate, darker
Watch out, wage them.

Deceit is real
Deceit is around,
Far and near, everywhere
Deceivers, green snakes
They live in and on green grasses,
Hunting down the unsuspecting
And the innocent.

FOCUS

Destiny is a focus
Focus on it.

Find the focus of your destiny
Focus on the destiny of your focus.

Destiny and focus, focus and destiny
Both are twins, unidentical.

Same, same, all round same
Lift your focus on destiny
Destroy other focuses against it.

Until you focus
You may not hit the target
Until you strike
Destiny will elude you.

Focus on destiny, all
For we are here for destiny
Destiny is mission
Mission is vision
The destined mission is accomplishable.

WAYWARDNESS

Waywardness never pays
Rather it harms.

Waywardness deludes reality
It entangles all debris
Gathering dirts along.

Waywardness blinds, blindfolding
It makes one live in darkness,
Staggering for vision
Struggling for sight.

Waywardness destroys
It is a bunch of irresponsibleness
None brags of it
None pride over it.

Waywardness is anti-destiny
It quashes and bashes it
It tackles and attacks it
Waywardness is a hater
Always bitter at destiny
Knowingly or unknowingly
Desist from it to fulfill destiny.

UPS AND DOWNS

Ups and downs are life
Life is about ups and downs
It flings you, rolls you
It cuddles you, abuses you.

Up and down is life
No matter who you are
It embraces you, pets you
It embarrasses you, harasses you.

Ups and downs is life
It accepts you, rejects you
Ups and downs is real
It hits you, beats you.

In life, in marriage
In education, in business
In job, in pastime
In health, in wealth
Ups and downs keep blowing.

Wait for them, prepare
Fight them, you may lose some
Endure them, they will pass
Win them, grab your destiny.

DIVINITY

Divinity is real
Great, greater than all
Assigning destinies.

Each man accordingly
Willingness depends
Readiness depends
But strength is given.

Divinity supports
Protecting the destined
Directing, controlling
Find out, align yourself.

Divinity patrols
Securing, availing
Find out, get in.

Divinity enhances
Harnessing, gathering
Refining and reforming
Tuning, fine-tuning the destined
Get up, join up, stay in, there.

ORDERLINESS

Destiny goes with order
And orderliness is the norm
Destiny orders, it orders
Yes, it really does.

When disorders come
When things scatter
When everyone is in disarray
When all is in shambles
Destiny whispers, order!

Orderliness keeps tracks
As destiny takes records
Orderliness moves in
As destiny steps up
Whatever happens, whenever
Destiny finds order in orderliness.

Be in order, in accordance
Always order your ways
For destiny finds peace there
Order, orderliness, steps, traces
All, and more buttress destiny.

Destiny can arrange disorder
It can also rearrange disorderliness,
Make yourself available
Always be on the lookout
Lest destiny gets disappointed.

HAND OF GOD

The hand of God
Mighty and heavy
Strong and rich,
Ready and willing
Eager and fit.

The hand of God
Gathering destinies
Picking them one by one
Sieving, separating
Putting them where they belong.

The hand of God
Healthy and wealthy
Balanced and perfect
Seeking, reaching out.

Sorting the destined
Setting them apart
Settling them on high
Planting them on fertile grounds
Watering and weeding
To satisfy Himself,
And feed the world.

DIRECTION

Direction is destiny
Destiny is direction,
Destiny directs
It directs the world.

Destiny follows directions
A specific direction for specific one
Patterned to arrive
Arrive at destination
Destination, true and great.

A destiny without direction
A direction without destiny,
None can survive it.

Find it, follow it, keep it on
The director is divine
March on, move on
Slow or fast, steadily
You will surely get there.

Direct destiny is on direction
Let no indirect lane fool you
Good luck, destiny's child
Destination is beckoning,
To bid you welcome.

ENEMIES

There are many enemies
They are in many forms
Some are friendly too.

Enemies like relatives
They are closer than ever
Enemies in the field
They want to take your place

Enemies, the real enemies
They are not hidden
They are not scared
They are ready to fight
They battle you openly and secretly
Just curious and furious.

Enemies that advance
Advance in manipulation
Methods, tactics, devices
They are just out to do harm
To devour and destroy.

Stay away, stay far
Be on guard, be vigilant
Stay gallant, fight on
Put them to flight.

FAKE FRIENDS

Fake friends on top
They barely help
 Fake friends in the middle
They castigate and gossip
Fake friends, down below
They wish evil always.

Fake friends, in and out
They only use and abuse
They lie, torment and torture
No contribution but pain.

Fake friends giving a greenlight
But bearers of redlight
They smile and laugh
But they plot evil,
They show beautiful face
But their heart is evil
Be careful, for destiny can be ruined
Yes, fake friends can kill.

Choose your friends
Mind yourself
Let the flow be real,
Listen to destiny
Let it lead you aright.

BETRAYERS

Betrayers kill
Even those that kiss you
Betrayers harm
Even those that watch over you,
Betrayers hurt
Even those that feed you.

They are many, too many
They look innocent
They appear poor too
And mild and meek
But they betray their masters.

Learn to not move with the crowd
Lest you lose your identity,
Destiny is an identity
Identity is destiny too.

Betrayers hide, they hide
You can hardly find them
Except miracles happen
Fear them, fear all, all
For none should be underestimated.

BAD RELATIVES

Bad relatives
In families, nuclear and extended
They pocknose and backbite.

They barely help
Even the destinies that are bright,
They neglect stars that shine
They avoid dreams and dreamers
Those that would bring them breakthrough.

Bad relatives, they live with you
They smile wider
They laugh louder
They play harder
Yet, they are mean
They deceive deeper.

Destinies suffer and starve
Sometimes because of them
Because of blind helpers
Due to adamant lifters,
Who vow not to contribute.

Define yourself, define your destiny
Work, and never look back
Hardly, would anyone help.

WRONG COMPANY

Wrong companies are ugly
They never beautify destiny,
Wrong companies defile
They tanish image.

Wrong companies blame
Rather than tame,
Wrong companies bring shame
Instead of fame,
They make one lame,
From dark game
If you seek a name
A good name at that
Flee from wrong company.

Men, women, old and young
Children, flee from them
Keep the faith, unflinching.

Wrong company is dangerous
Deadlier than poison
Never keep them, never be one
Destiny forbids wrong company.

FAMILY OUTRAGE

Family is good
God, made it so
Family is natural
God made it original,
We bond, we relate
We are inseparable
Nature tied us together.

So when we tend to deviate
When we misbehave
When we fall sick
Even when we succeed,
Family is always there.

So it is, when otherwise
When we pull out
When we discover strange destiny
When we appear like the prodigal son,
Or vagabond or black sheep
Family rages, outrageously.

But then, destiny cares not
Sometimes destiny is blunt
It gives us more sacred duty
That we do the unthinkable.

Destiny is lone
It is bold,
No one stops it
Nor stands on its way,
Destiny can abandon whoever.

MADNESS

Destiny comes with force
It hammers greatly
It bursts like balloon
And explodes like bomb
Whoever fails to submit
May become subdued.

Destiny can cause madness
Hallucination and lunatic-ism
Mental and psychological
Emotional and spiritual trauma.

Call it madness, or not
Call it anything, whatever
Destiny can take any route
To arrive at its tale.

Avoid disobedience
Follow its track
Trace the footprints,
Plant your footsteps,
Let the mark be seen
Even if they call it madness
Otherwise the real madness may begin.

RESTLESSNESS

Destiny comes with a pang
Like a woman in labour
Panting in trivails
To be delivered of her baby
To give life, new life.

Destiny is pregnancy
Neither hidden nor restful
In it are dreams and realities,
Destiny bears futures
Futures of generations
Generations unborn, unknown.

It causes restlessness
It gives none, peace
Nothing interests or satisfies
Until destiny is born.

Bear it, born it, feed it
Nurse it, nurture and tend it
For only then can rest come
Destiny is a calling
To answer a call,
Sometimes you may not be prepared,
But then you must answer
Because destiny is also a call
To answer for a people yet uncalled.

INTEREST

Interest is a signal
It always has something to say,
Although our interest may not be it
But chances tell that interests are destinies.

Nothing interests, no interest
Except where destiny is
Destiny is jealous
Destiny is loud,
Destiny is domineering
Destiny is possessive
It is obsessive,
No matter what else we seek.

For your interest and your passion
For your love, that one thing
That one that makes you sleepless
It keeps you awake
Gives you happiness and sadness
That one that calms your nerves
Pick it up, that is it.

Keep digging it, dig it deeper
It may be gold,
You, your gold, your raw gold
Dig it up, refine it
You would be refined, including the world.

LOVE

Destiny is love, true love
It is the only love, real
It hates you not
Nor ever leaves you
Destiny defines pure love
The only love that stays
It neither grows dim
Nor fluctuates.

Destiny loves, love it
Destiny cares, care for it
Destiny grooms, groom it
Destiny sees, see it, through it
Destiny tames, tame it.

Destiny realizes, realize it, for it
Destiny summons, summon it
Destiny watches, watch it
It guides, guide it.

Destiny guards, guard it
It spreads, spread it
Love destiny truly and really
The world will gather at your feet.

WANTS AND NEEDS

Wants are vast
Together with needs
They grow daily
Yes, with inventions.

Wants are large
Together with needs,
They spread steadily
Yes, with innovations.

Science and technology
Findings, researches
Productions and creations
All and more widen it all.

Destiny overlooks wants
Destiny shuns needs
Because destiny is want
And destiny is need,
Whether we like it or not.

Sometimes, destiny fights
Yes, it fights wants and needs
Because they may chance it.

Know your wants
Separate them from your needs,
Make sure they point at destiny
Lest, you sell it out.

STRUGGLE

The struggle is real
Because life is a big struggle
The struggle is a jungle
And not all are lions.

Hence, destiny is a lion
Wallowing in the jungle,
Fighting to survive
Trying to stay alive
Roaring to be the leader.

The struggle is hard
Sometimes it appears lost
The struggle is heavy
Not all can carry it
It is a yoke
Around the neck,
Only destiny bears it.

Struggle with destiny
The destined has a struggle
See that you win
Because the ordained cannot lose.

Ngozi Olivia Osuoha

SERIOUSNESS

Destiny is serious
It is a serious business
It never gets less.

Destiny involves seriousness
Because without it, it will not happen.

Destiny deals with serious people
Because unto them, it survives.

Seriousness must be there
For destiny to be serious.

Destiny does not cut corners
Neither does it dupe
Destiny avoids pranks and pranksters
And leaves tricksters out,
Because it is a certainty.

Destiny is not cruel
It befriends the poor,
And welcomes the rich
Destiny is seriously calm.

Be serious, run for destiny
Win for it, you are the winner
You can do it, seriously.

DETERMINATION

Determination is life
Because life is hard,
Determined people climb the world
They fear not the mountain
Irrespective of the scariness.

Determination lifts destiny
As destiny leans on determination.

The determinants of destiny are much
But you must be determined,
In the face of difficulty
On the scale of hardship
On the tray of hate
In the show of bitterness,
Envy, anger, jealousy
Destiny determines no going back.

Determination succeeds
It wins the race
No matter the losses
Despite failures and fears
Irrespective of the doubts
Destiny marries determination.

Ngozi Olivia Osuoha

WATERING

Life needs water
Spring, stream, river, ocean
Mist, dew, fog, rain.

Water is a natural resource
Which helps life,
Water is very necessary
Vital, to all, in all.

Destiny needs water
Waters that never dry
Destiny depends on water
Watered destiny outgrows others.

Watered destiny blossoms
It shines, booms and blooms
It is rich, young, green
Always fresh and lively.

Watering destinies means a lot
Prayers, works, empowerment
Loyalty, support, love, care
Correction, platforms, push
Supply, placement and many more,
So water your destiny
Keep watering, even when you arrive.

LEARNING

Learning is life
It is from the beginning
It never ends.

Learning advances
In forms unfathomable,
Learning pierces, penetrates
It goes beyond borders.

Learning helps, it digs
It unearths, it levels
Learning provides, produces
It harnesses and harvests.

Learning is destiny
Destiny is learning
Unique, technical, great
It baffles, marvels, wonders.

Learn, learn, unlearn, relearn
Keep moving, keep running, keep it
Destiny has a lot to learn
Just as it has a lot to teach.

Ngozi Olivia Osuoha

GROWING

We grow from birth
We grow till death,
We grow, we just keep growing.

Growth is an assignment
No matter how natural it may be,
Growth is an obligation
As necessary as it is
Growth is a force
As unseen as it is
Growth plunders barriers.

Growth summons courage
It overcomes darkness
And conquers backwardness
Growth hunts for tomorrow
And haunts the past.

Destiny is growth
It requires growth,
It forestalls growth
It manifests growth
It labours for growth,
And harbours same
Destiny nourishes growth.

DISCOVERY

Discovery is part of creation
Discovery is a ship,
It sails the waters
From coast to coast
In diverse currents
Encountering storms and waves
Yet, carrying on, great.

Discovery is long
It lingers, it enlongates
Linking the past, present and future,
Intertwining them together.

Discovery discovers destiny
And destiny is a discovery.

Discover destiny, destinies and destinations
Destinations enroute,
Enroute the creator.

Discovered destiny is beautiful
Its wonders never cease to amaze,
Discovered destinies discover others
Together, they lift the world.

FORWARD MOVEMENT

Destiny moves forward
No matter what it faces,
Destiny never looks back
No matter what it forgot,
Destiny keeps moving
Despite the past.

Forward movement helps
Yes, destiny on the move
Going up, higher still.

Even at odd times
When things seem gloomy
When the way is dark
When no light seems to shine,
Destiny marks time,
Waiting to launch into the deep
With a full force.

Troubles taunt it
Problems shake it
Loopholes question it
Mistakes mock it,
Yet, destiny on the rise.

If it stops accidentally
If it cools mistakenly
With time, it regains power
Gathering heavier momentum,
Suddenly, it will awake
In a twinkle, it flies
Covering up, making up
Picking all it ever lost in glory.

RAPE

Rape is a crime
Against God and humanity
Rape is an abuse
It is ungodly and unholy
Anybody can fall victim,
Man, woman, boy, girl, child
It can happen anywhere.

Rape kills, it torments
It is a torture, a sin
The trauma is unthinkable.

Rape affects destiny
Some survive it
Some do not
Some move on, some die
Some even commit suicide,
Some die from the shock
And the heartbreak from disappointment,
Yes, disappointment from their God
Or whatever they held dear.

Never rape, rape no destiny
Carnally or otherwise
Discipline cuts across sex
Urges are tamed, cautioned
Destiny abhors rape
Humanity and God, do too.

ACCIDENT

There are many types of accident
Physical and spiritual inclusive
Physical, hurts our body
Spiritual, hurts our spirit.

Sometimes, physical are seen
They may do no harm,
Sometimes, spiritual are not seen
And they do more harm.

Disruption of destinies
Killing of gifts
Suppression of destinies
Assassination of voices,
These and more are accidents too.

They frustrate dreams
And tamper with futures,
They terminate some
And erase many,
Destiny can be killed by accident as well
They can be met or harnessed
They can be discovered accidentally too.

WITCHCRAFT AND WIZARDRY

There are forces everywhere
Forces, good and bad
Forces that control and confine
They manipulate, maneuver.

These forces can be odd
They can be ungodly, evil
They can be mean, rude
They are out solely to destroy.

They destroy, they dismantle
They scatter, they shatter
They are wicked and heartless
They never care,
Some are assigned against dreams.

Witches and wizards, evil spirits
They fight destinies, they fight
They bend on crushing them
But there is a God of destinies
That grants means of escape.

Destinies win,
No matter the forces
When powers that be, clash
Victory rejoices with destiny.

HATE

Hate is real, very real
From the word, go
Hate is strong, very strong
It can raze homes.

Hate is strict, hard
It penetrates walls
Hate is evil
It does barbaric things.

Hate permeates layers
Layers of generations
Born, unborn, known, unknown
Hate is a greedy force.

Destinies suffer hate
Hated destinies suffer
They face more foes
They battle more wars
And see more troubles
But blessed destinies always shine.

Destiny is divine
Link to divinity,
Let your steps be divinely guarded.

WICKEDNESS

Wickedness is a tool
An evil tool against people
A tool used by evil ones
To suffer people even unjustly.

Wickedness does not pay
Instead, it does wrong
Nothing good comes from it
Rather destruction and ugliness.

Wickedness favours no one
No matter how it is used
Wickedness mutilates destinies
Even when sane and sound.

Wickedness seeks only revenge
Revenge even without offense
Wickedness splits peace
Planting discord,
Wickedness hates destinies.

Do not be wicked
It does more harm
Be happy and do good,
Forgive, let go
Live and let live
The world is a stage.

GOSSIP

Gossip, a story of joblessness
A talk of bare emptiness
Murmurings, offsides
Musings of busybodies.

Gossips, finger destiny
They point accusing fingers
Searching for reasons
Looking for loopholes.

Gossip is a vain word
It holds no water
Real or fake, true or false
Gossip is just for cowards.

Destinies hate gossip
The destined do not gossip
They tell truths, truths all the time.

Stay away from gossip
Gossiping can paint black
Even when white is spotless
Destiny is so divine.

SCANDAL

Scandals, the pivot of pain
The angles of trauma
And the shapes of anger.

Scandals, ruin reputation
They forge terrible stories
They cook ugly news
Spreading them like wildfires.

But destiny progresses
Finding way to be free
Advancing, no matter what.

Scandalizers make money sometimes
They fan ambers of trouble
Sharing bad thoughts
Dishing silly notions,
Writing horrible notes.

Scandals torment destinies
But destinies outsmart them,
Words are powerful
They are weightier than sounds
Refrain from useless words
Let your words be meaningful,
Because careless talks do more harm.

RUMOUR

Rumourmongers are crude
No matter how sophisticated,
They rumour and clamour
Adding glamour and flavour
Just to get favour,
After tarnishing images.

Numerous rumours are lies
Propagandas of heavy weights
Just to inflict pain
For indictment, and selfish gains
To gather unnecessary attention
To chase away help and helpers, sometimes.

Rumours, crazy rumours
Rumourmongers, crazy rumourmongers
Hateful, vengeful, devilish
They deduce deviations
They bargain losses
They profit from them all.

Little or nothing, much or most
Temporary, it last
Stay away from destinies
Let them blossom
For their assignment is much.

Rumours pay no holiness
They do doom and evil,
Be good and live upright
Face your life and future,
Let your destiny not be rumormongering.

BLACKMAIL

The blackmailer jubilates
Celebrating dubious feat
Toasting to heartbreak.

Blackmails, gainless, needless
Yet, they are bent on it
Bent on erasing destiny.

Blackmails puncture destiny
They rupture it as well
They even capture it
But destiny is destined.

Black mail sent to destiny
A destiny not black,
A mail so black
To destroy a clean destiny.

Say no to blackmails
Stay away from frame-ups
Allow destiny to shine
For in its shine lies light
The light that will counter darkness.

ILLITERACY

Illiteracy is deadly
It is also a poison
It can be that harmful.

Illiteracy corks destiny
It never allows it glitter
No matter how it strives.

Illiteracy is cunning
It can take a lead
Moving speedily
Yet lagging behind.

Be enlightened, embrace change
Get trained, link up
Let destiny spread out.

Destiny fights illiteracy
Just same way illiteracy fights it
Destiny begets life.

POVERTY

It has killed many
Poverty is a devil
It deceives,
Poverty is bad
It can cause stillbirth.

Dreams die, visions doom
Missions collapse, passions quench
Because of poverty.

Poverty is an enemy
An arch-rival, great beast
It blocks success.

Poverty hinders movement
It arrests growth and development,
Poverty can make one sick
It shatters destinies.

Fight poverty, conquer it
Win it, triumph over it
For destiny needs not be poor.

ROADBLOCKS

Roadblocks, big and small
High and low
Artificial and natural
Manmade and circumstantial.

Roadblocks to destiny
Roadblocks against destiny
Roadblocks in destiny
Too many of them.

Look, yonder and within
Look, look before you leap
Watch, watch and pray
For the wrestling is tough.

Below and above
All round roadblocks
Choose wisely and carefully
Select calmly and consciously
Cross over, run the race
For destiny is not alone.

FRUSTRATIONS

Frustrations like a cup of tea
Frustrations like daily bread
Food, water, clothing
Frustrations on the path of destiny.

Study, belief, want, need
Dream, wish, desire, aim
Checks and balances
Frustrations always on them all.

Hidden, some, sometimes
Unhidden, some, sometimes
Visible, invisible
Yet destiny is invincible.

Strong destinies retaliate
They retreat and reinforce
They never surrender.

Frustrations camp around
They follow destinies about
They vow to destroy and kill
But be strong, lean on God.

ABANDONMENT

Abandonment, yes, very well
Sometimes, destinies are abandoned
Friends and families do
Colleagues and mentors do
Well-wishers run, supporters hide
Destinies move on, lone and weary.

Heavy destinies weigh down
Bearers stumble and stagger
Gigantic destinies get discouraged
Carriers faint and fail
Abandonment looms.

Destinies choke and suffocate
Destinies give up and mourn
Destinies go sobber and cool
Destinies burn down and off.

But destinies awake, reawaken
They violently take it by force
They put up strengths in all
Capturing, winning, celebrating
Flying higher everyday.

DISOWN

Some get disowned
Some get rejected
As they lament boredom
Loneliness flogs them
As they weep for help
Pains humiliate them.

Destinies are funny
They are weird and odd
They hardly fit in
Because they are exceptional.

Until they break through
Until they get recognized
Until they shatter the ceiling
No one takes them serious.

Even parents threaten them
Siblings avoid them sometimes
They talk and act strange
Because they are true strangers.

But all return, claiming peace
Beckoning fraternity when the road becomes crystal,
When destiny wins
When breakthroughs get lauded.

LONELINESS

Destinies are bored
They go lonely, alone
They stay in the cave
Cave of discoveries
Cave of cleansing
Cave of ordination
Cave of consecration
And that of sacredness.

Pure cave, cave of holiness
They separate themselves
Until a certain time
They announce themselves
In a given line.

Loneliness is attached to destiny
Destiny goes with self
It discovers a whole lot
Then it serves the world.

Loneliness is diverse
Being alone is not feeling lonely
Because destiny is more than an army.

Solitude is a page
A phase, a gap
A necessary valley that must be passed
For mountains to be climbed
Mountains of fantastic destinations.

DEPRESSION

Destiny can cause depression
Yes, it can
Destiny can cure depression
Yes, it can
It depends on time.

Unknown destiny causes trouble
The search for it, causes pain
Yearning for discovery; pains
Until then, nothing works really.

Discovered destiny gives joy
It breaks limits, strongholds
Found destiny is cherished
Irrespective of strange voices.

Destiny fights depression
Because depression challenges it
Destiny is purpose
Purpose is destiny
Both are reasons
Reasons to be here
Find it, find them, live them.

ABUSE

Abuse is sure
Abuse from home and abroad
Families and friends
All round, every corner.

Verbal, physical, mental
Career, societal, marital
Until abuse becomes normal.

Destiny learns from abuse
Abuse does not support it
Destiny dislikes abuse though
But abuse hates destiny.

Abuse is bad
It is a crime,
Nothing abused, feels alright
But then, life must go on.

Abuse nothing
Abuse no one,
Let no one abuse you
But expect it, just in case.

Abuse climbs towers, many
Singing ugly songs of war
Chanting division and horror
But destiny watches from below.

Abuse separates, segregates
Fomenting trouble and shame
Desecrating destinies in full force
But destiny remains sacred.

Altars speak, altars fight
They drag, they collide
They war, they fight
Altars opposite, counter
But never equal,
They elevate destiny
And raise them from the gutters.

Then abuse gives way
Feeling ashamed,
Because what will be, will be.

FOOL

Destiny can be foolish
And can make one, foolish
Yes, destiny sounds awkward
And also absurd
Especially to blind people.

Destiny forces fools to fool you
Because of its strangeness
Destiny speaks in different voices
And raises eyebrows,
Destiny appears silly
And makes silliness out of one
But when it breaks forth
The proclaimed fool becomes lord.

They call you fool, capital fool
They fool you, treat you like fool
They advise, caution and ban
But destiny insists, resists, persists
Because there is a great destination.

Be fool to walk and work alone
Be foolish enough to understand,
Because destiny is not a fool.

But be sure you are not actually a fool
Let the foolishness be of destiny,
Because destiny cannot be a fool
Irrespective of how foolish they see it.

DOUBTS AND SELF DOUBTS

Doubts arise from all corners
Questioning the possibility
Self doubts mount pressures
Weighing the authenticity.

Doubts, doubting all
Self doubts doubting strengths
Complicated chances and fate
Complex fears and discouragement.

Definite destiny doubting
Indefinite destiny confusing
Defined destinations unseen
Clear paths yet unknown
Fears and factors forcing down.

Yes, doubts kill destinies
Self doubts, double-kills them
But one bold step is enough
Enough to make it happen.

Live it real, big or small
Grab it with all your might
Weak or strong, destiny pushes on.

UNWANTED

Yes, unwanted you may be
Unloved, undesired, uncared for
Unvalued, unpleasant, unchosen
Because your destiny is funny.

Crazy destiny bearers act crazily
They do weird things
They pass through ugly situations
And encounter strangest circumstances,
Be ready, be strong, never quit
Because the tunnel is the channel.

No matter how unwanted you may be
Despite the shortcomings
No matter the odds against you
Destiny is stubborn,
It always finds its way.

So hang in there, though they pursue you
Hold on, though they chase you away
Be consistent, though you hunger and thirst
For a day is near, a day of unveiling
A day of your launching into the world.

HELPLESS

Help hardly comes
Even with evidences,
Help barely lasts
Even when needed,
Help hides and flies
Even at dying point
So face yourself, real
Look away from help.

They come to castigate
They come to mock
They come to laugh and scorn
They come to distract
They are just there to challenge,
Hardly, do they come for good
But let all those spur you.

Helpless destinies survive too
Because their maker is alive
Never be discouraged
Destiny is destined
Blessed and consecrated
Anointed to face the world
Go forth in that unction
You have divine speed,
You will succeed and exceed expectations.

Ngozi Olivia Osuoha

CONFUSION

Sometimes, there will be confusion
Sometimes, great trouble
Confusion to choose, to stand
To obey, to continue
Yes, great dilemma
But keep on keeping on.

Confusion in the family
Confusion at work, in work, for work
Confusion within and without
Personal and general confusion,
As why you do what you do
And the necessity, need.

Advance, once sure of it
Continue, if convinced
Carry on, tomorrow is green
For only you know the weight you bear
And the load on your shoulders.

Do not give in to confusion
March on, soldier of destiny
Your destination beckons
A welcome feast awaits,
A banquet of victory.

BANDWAGON

The bandwagon is always there
With so much noise
Heating up the airwaves
Scattering sounds all over
Lauding unnecessary things,
But beware of them
And mindful of who you are.

Bandwagons, trains of noise
Locomotives, chambers of nuisance
Dragging many along
Even in a cross country
Many being caught up in the marathon
Deafening marathons
Tiring, tiresome, and wasteful
Pulling muscles of powerless ones
And even the powerful.

See them, look beyond them all
Avoid them, drive yours
For destiny is not a bandwagon.

Desist from noise and noisemakers
For they roll many a time in loss
Gather moss, gather knowledge
Gather wisdom, for destiny is a pack of wisdom.

PEER PRESSURE

Peer pressure, pressure of peer
Piercing the milkiness of flesh
Devouring originality and poorness
Restructuring life negatively at times.

Peer pressure, it kills, it does
Many have died from it
Young fellows, ignorant
Running to meet death
They play hide and seek
They trick and prank
Helplessly loud and around
Mesmerizing themselves in folly
Thinking otherwise in enjoyment.

Poor brains, meek minds, tenderness
Doing crazy and stupid things
Learning fast, evil ways
Digging graves for themselves
Because they feel arrived
Or it is their time to play.

Destiny fears peer pressure
Peer pressure kills destiny
Beware of your environment
Be careful with your friends
Let your groups keep you safe
If they must be there.

DOGMAS

Dogmas abound, yes
They are everywhere
Especially dogmas of old,
Those of the quiet past.

They see today, and tomorrow
With the eyes of old
The eyes of dogmatic bones.

Let them not fool you
Their deceit is harmful,
Intentionally or unintentionally
Avoid them, for they are strict,
Restricted and restrictive.

Their inflexibility is second to none
Their inagility is dangerous
Times have changed
Times are still changing,
Yet they know not.

Around them is stiffness
Move on with flexibility
Let your agility make way for you,
For destiny is dynamic too.

MENTALITY

Mentality is another thing
It helps deal with destiny,
Whether for or against.

Mentality is the base
It is also a seatbelt
It controls a lot,
And saves much
It works wonders.

Positive mentality grows
Negative mentality dwindles
Both affect destiny same.

Work on your head
Flourish your mindset
Enlarge your heart,
Purify your soul
Cleanse your spirit
Santify your body
They would develop your destiny.

Rich mentality booms destiny
But not stupidity,
Poor mentality dries it
But not silliness,
Water your mentality
Let your destiny be watered.

TABOO

When you are strange
When you are abnormal,
When you are not regular
When you are not an everyday person
They call you names.

When there is a god in you
An Oracle to be heard
A road to be followed,
They tag you, possessed.

They call it taboos
When you cross boundaries, theirs
Boundaries of common men
Uncommon areas and places
They say it is a tabbo.

When you see possibilities
When you create choices
When you trade on scorpions
And control forces, strange forces
They say you are a spirit.

They will fight you down
They will do a lot,
They will try a whole lot
But be you, for you are just one you.

Ngozi Olivia Osuoha

BROKE

Destinies may not be rich
In fact, they may never be
Destinies may dwell in hardship
In fact, it is never easy
But it does not belittle them.

They are voices, heroes
They are legends, giants
Whether rich or poor
Whether famous or unknown
Their duty towards man
And their duty towards God
All, make them destined.

Broke, broken and lack
Want, need, poorness and poverty
Troubles, traumas, pain, shame
All and many more, never stop them.

Fear not when you are broke
Worry less when you are hungry
Ask less questions why it is so
For destiny supersedes flesh
And callings surpass human.

CONNECTIONS AND GODFATHERS

Destiny suffers a lot
Especially when unhelped
Destiny gets discouraged
Mostly, when alone
Destiny cries, mourns
Because of many things
But destiny is only human.

Connections help a lot
Godfathers pave ways too,
Especially in the right directions.

Humans are there to help each other
People are meant to save one another
Support goes a long way
Love and care too, do
No man survives alone
No one is an island,
Humans need humans.

Destinies with connections and godfathers
Go far, farther, further and better
It takes special grace to outshine them.

Struggle, work on dear
Even without connections
When there are no godfathers
Remember, there is the greatest destiny helper
The one who actually gives it.

FAVOUR AND FAME

Destiny connects to favour
When destiny is excellent or potential
Destiny creates fame
When it is great,
Favoured destiny is blessed
Because it goes viral
Local, national, international.

Destiny brings favour, yes
Polish it, sell it, display it
Choose to be favoured
Whether possible or not.

Fame is a good thing
But not all fame is worth it
Favour garnishes destiny
Destiny oils fame.

But fame is vanity
Destiny is never
Be real, be courageous, not desperate
Work, show your work
For destiny can never be cheated.

DECISION

Decision is critical
Decisions peg us
Squarely, circularly or anyhow.

Decisions bounce back
They go forward as well
Decisions interfere, intertwine
Good ones, move up
Bad ones, fall down
Good ones, bad ones can crisscross
Still good ones have their ways
Whether we win or lose
They do affect us.

Consciousness helps too
Courage pays as well
Confidence exaults
Decide wisely, pray too
Not all decisions are made alone
Consult people in some cases
Wise ones, confidants
Good luck on your destiny.

SCALE OF PREFERENCE

Scale of preference
Yes, this scale that prefers and refers
Proffering solutions sometimes.

Scale of preference
Learn to choose
Yes, choose from all
Let the box be opened
All the probabilities, in it.

Scale them, all, one by one
Critically analize them
Purposes, times, needs, sizes
Chances, reasons, seasons
Pray over them, make a wish
Let the weight tell.

Preference may not be the scale
The scale may not be the preference,
But other factors are there
Distribute their weights equally
Let them pass the judgement
Destiny judges also, beware.

PRIORITY

Priority helps a lot
It saves more also.

Priorities sieve, they gather
Priorities waste not
When gotten right.

Priorities, one by one
But be it, in order
According to time and purse
Prudence and management
Priorities mother everything.

Priority differs with men
It appears less or more with time
A priority fades also
It can magnify its lens.

Get your priorities right
Screen them, pick them
Clean, clear, neat, pure
They help destinies glow
Destiny is a priority,
A major one
That should not be toiled with.

ODDS AND PURPOSE

There are many odds
Especially those against purpose
Odds can frustrate
They discourage actually.

When odds are high
Chances dim and reduce,
When odds are real
Necessities slim down.

Odds against purpose
Purpose to terminate destiny
But destiny is a purpose,
It purposes, to fights for its purpose
And also purposes, proposes to stay on course.

Odds grow too, they lessen as well
Odds come from anywhere
Humans, forces, factors
Seen, unseen, known, unknown
Odds are mean, determined
Only the determined win odds,
Especially against odds and beyond odds.

Purpose, to fulfill your purpose
Because the purpose of destiny dares not die.

BREAKTHROUGH

Destiny is a breakthrough
Its prime purpose is freedom
Breakthrough is a destiny
It yields not to death,
Except otherwise.

Destiny breaks through
It brings breakthrough
Destiny breaks breakthrough
For everything to go through.

The destiny of breakthrough is great
It calls for celebration
It speaks beyond worlds
And passes through walls.

Breakthrough is freedom
It liberates the people
It gives them hope
And emancipates them.

Let destiny be heard
Let it be felt, seen, celebrated
For nothing ever beats a blessed destiny.

Ngozi Olivia Osuoha

VOICE

You are a voice
A great voice to be heard,
So speak, let them listen.

You are a voice, voice of destiny
Speak, shout, sing, hum
Whisper, let destiny hear too.

You are a destined voice
Let the world know
Speak, speak, and keep speaking.

Destiny is a voice
No matter the form,
Destiny is a song
No matter the tune,
Destiny is a sound
No matter the medium,
Destiny travels far and wide
Spreading to all parts of the earth.

Speak, on top of your voice
They must hear, they must listen
Even if they hate you
Though they wish not to,
Destiny cannot be silenced
Let the enemy be put to shame.

You carry more than gold
The world cannot unearth you,
Show, display, play, dance
This work is compulsory
Lest, souls perish.

FORGONE ALTERNATIVE

Opportunity cost, yes!
Destiny is an opportunity
Opportunity to serve,
Service to mankind, humanity and God.

It has a cost, a big one
No matter the assignment,
Despite the volume or style.

Destiny is a call to worship
Serve, save humanity
No alternative, no option.

It is destiny or nothing
There is no forgone alternative.

Face destiny, will it, do it
Win the world, win big
No room for a forgone alternative.

Opportunity tells of cost,
Cost tells of opportunity
Opportunities and costs are vast
They both, go hand in hand.

Opportunity cost, yes it is
Opportunity cost, cost in all
Opportunity is the cost of destiny
Destiny is the opportunity cost,
It is the destined cost
And a costly opportunity,
As Opportunity cost is the forgone alternative
So, Destiny is just the opportunity,
Not forgone, not alternative
None, no alternative to be forgone.

Ngozi Olivia Osuoha

Destiny

Ngozi Olivia Osuoha is a Nigerian poet, writer and thinker. A graduate of Estate Management with experience in Banking and Broadcasting.

She has eighteen poetry books published in Kenya, Canada, the Philippines, USA, and others. She has also co-authored one (with Kenyan literary critic Amos O. Ojwang').

She has been featured in over sixty-five international anthologies and also has published over two hundred and fifty poems and articles in over twenty countries.

Many of her poems have been translated and published into other languages, including Spanish, Russian, Romanian, Polish, Khloe, Farsi, and Arabic, among others.

She has won many awards; she is a one time *Best of the Net* nominee, and she has numerous words on marble.

www.ingramcontent.com/pod-product-compliance
Lightning Source LLC
Chambersburg PA
CBHW020141130526
44591CB00030B/173